*A tribute to the limerick and lovers of craic*

# There once was a book, to be sure

# Dr X

**To contact the author, or to check out the author's
other books, visit www.vividpublishing.com.au/drx**

Copyright © 2017 Fingerprint Communications NSW Pty Ltd (Australia)

ISBN: 978-1-925590-34-0

Published by Vivid Publishing
P.O. Box 948, Fremantle
Western Australia 6959
www.vividpublishing.com.au

Cataloguing-in-publication data is held at the National Library of Australia

All rights reserved. No part of this publication may be reproduced, stored in a retrieval system or transmitted in any form or by any means, electronic, mechanical, photocopying, recording or otherwise, without the prior written permission of the copyright holder.

**DEDICATED TO LOVERS OF CRAIC**

Let it no longer be maligned as the red-headed stepchild of the snoberati, for the limerick is beloved by millions.

Among the fine masses it is warmly embraced. So it is time to put things right, and bring our friend back to the fold.

A hearty companion to any day. From the park to the pub, and all the way from here to Nantucket.

A tonic to lift the spirits and, mercifully, not always politically correct.

Welcome back dear limerick. It's been too long.

**LIMERICK SHOT DOWN IN THE 'P-C SALOON'**

Three people walked into the bar,
A Madam, the Pope, and the Tsar,
The *'Keep* looked at me:
"Sorry, just gone P-C ...
"I'd suggest this won't get very far!"

## DA LIMERICK IS IN DA HOUSE – 2BSURE 2BSURE

To be sure, it's right that it's time to have fun,
A good dose of *Silly* will clear up this glum,
Let's bring back the limerick,
('Cos the news is just *so* sick)
And we'll do our best to rhyme things with bum!

## THERE ONCE WAS A LIMERICK ...
## DOWN WITH WORD SNOBS

The poor limerick is sadly maligned,
As a cheap and a cheesy old rhyme,
But with just the right zing,
Man, these things can sing,
Delivering *joy* in most every line.

Yes, until now, the artform's declined,
Blame Word Snobs - who pretend they're refined,
But they wouldn't know fun,
If it bit 'em on the bum*,
So don't feel guilty – we don't want their time!

\*Mission accomplished

**THE STRAY DIGIT DILEMMA**

The teacher was found guilty of being too loose,
For his triangle was not deemed obtuse,
But we found (and what luck!),
A stray digit *stuck*,
Right there – up his hypotenuse!

**DARLINK DEVINE**

Darlink Devine was a true fashion mainstay,
They'd all wear whatever she would say,
She'd look down at a gown,
Give a horrible frown,
And shriek "*Oh no!!!* ... it's simply last Wednesday!"

**HUFFER THE PUFFER**

Henry Huffer had such shocking bad breath,
That he'd still 'linger' long after he'd left,
His poor wife couldn't smell,
Which is really just as well,
Otherwise offspring would have meant IVF.

**THE BUTTON HOLE MASSACRE**

Beer Belly Bob had a shirt under humongous strain,

An army tent *tailored* to cover his frame,

But with that last stroganoff,

A button wildly shot off,

Killing poor Clarrie - just in off the lane.

**HAPPY AUDIENCE**

There once was a bombshell, Patricia,
Who was really the fabulous stripper.
Her fond clientelle,
Included Sergeant McKell,
The headmaster, the Mayor, and the Vicar.

**THE MODERN BLOKE JOKE**

*"You are sexiest and you are demeaning!"*,
Leered the Prof with the feminist leaning.
Is this some kind of joke?
I'm just a regular bloke.
Wired for *fun* - not your judgemental preening.

## PERU, MAGOO, YOU'VE DONE IT AGAIN

There was an old man from Peru,
Whose name was Pablo Magoo,
Got his glasses 'at cost',
Last we heard, he was lost,
Somewhere atop of Machu Picchu!

## MESSAGE IN A BOTTLE

There was a shipwreck survivor called Hearst,
Not heard from since back on the 1st,
A note bobbed about,
And when finally fished out,
Said: *"Send more bottles – we're dying of thirst!"*.

## TOBY

There was a young lad know as Toby,
To the Parental Polis he was 'known-ski',
At the sound of a crash,
*Away* he would dash,
(Being a boy can be thankless and lonely!)

**HOOKED**

There was a retired gent known as Ken,
Who preferred to be fishing by 10,
With the right bait on his hook,
A fine trout he'd soon cook,
Then be hungry to get out there again.

**THE LINE MARKER**

There was a line marker called Fraser,
Who did his very best work with a laser,
But things went astray,
With the hiccups that day,
Thank goodness he's back now ... with an eraser.

**YOU SAW NOTHING**

There was a fine lass by the name of Patrice,
Who just happened to be *Da Boss's* niece,
So at 'The Blue Show 'n Tell',
She was known as Shontelle.
That's *real* witness protection – capiche?!

## NYE AND LOW

There was an intrepid surgeon called Nye,
Who looked down low (then looked way up high).
Then he bought an X-ray,
And we all heard him say:
"*Ah!* There's more to this than first meets the eye."

**A SURE BET**

Here's a hot tip and I'll give it for free,
The bet of the week. A fait accompli.
Whatever I back,
Get *off* that damned hack.
It'll run *fourth* - just you wait and see!

**McWHIRTER's BLURTER**

This is the tale of Albert McWhirter,
Who had trouble controlling his blurter,
At the mere sound of a toot,
His poor wife would scoot,
Out for fresh air - so nothing could hurt her.

**HARRIET'S CHARIOT**

There was an old duck we knew as dear Harriet,

Who, once a year, would go out in her chariot.

12 clicks an hour she'd go,

*She didn't consider it slow,*

Which may explain how she 'checked in' at the Marriott.

**THE ELECTION REFLECTION**

There once was a skilled politician,
Came out firing, with all ammunition,
Into power he swept,
Not a promise was kept ...
*This is a tale worthy of high repetition.*

**ROSE 'N THE HOSE**

There once was a lady called Rose,
Who could suck a ball right through a hose.
When asked of her fandom,
Her guess was quite random:
*"Me happy demeanour, I s'pose."*

**HITTING THE FAN**

They welcomed a new boss, across there in Perth,
And it must be said, he had quite the girth.
When he threw his weight round,
They all went to ground,
So what *hit the fan* ... was purely just dirt!

**BAD LAW McGRAW**

There once was a cop named McGraw,
Who, sadly, strayed outside the law,
He was caught on the take,
Putting files in a cake,
So now he lives - *over there* - in Cell Four.

**TROUBLE AHOY**

The bank manager said: You'd better move fast,
It looks like the die's already been cast,
The loan will not float,
They've reclaimed the boat,
And they've run a white flag up the mast!

**GO AHEAD, MAKE MY CHIPS**

There was a Swat Cop known as Driscoll,
Who was incredibly skilled with his pistol,
He could shoot a stray hair,
Off the end of a chair,
While eating hot chips by the fistful.

## ME ENORMOUS LABOURUS

Oi! They gave me a task so enormous,
It weren't even there in me thesaurus,
But I chipped and I chopped,
Then I heaved, and I lopped,
Behold!  Me Opus Labourus.

**CONTENDER PRETENDER**

As the glamour sweeps in for a contender,
It's clear I'm the utter pretender.
I'm fat and I'm old,
I'm covered in mould,
But I've got a pulse ... and, by God, *I remember!*

## FOR WHOM THE FEE TOLLS

To get where I needed to be,
It was nothing but toll roads for me,
But each beep of my tag,
Meant my savings would sag.
So now I'm *'walking off'* a big bleepin' fee.

**THE SHOW 'N TELL HOTEL**

Our hotels are like Russian Roulette,
You simply don't know what you're going to get,
From the fridge to the shower,
It's time for guest power:
The Geneva Convention ... *of what to expect!*

**CARPARK LAMENT**

Deep down into the carpark I descend,
The ghoulish prices only found at the end,
It's too far to reverse,
These fees are perverse,
So I must sell the car before ten!

**PIN-NESIA**

In order to protect my own wealth,
I have pin codes – for cunning and stealth,
But so many I've gotten,
My memory's turned rotten,
And I've run out of food on the shelf.

**THE SUBLIME THREE-FIFTY-NINE**

There was a bus: The Three-Fifty-Nine,
That would *never* be running to time.
It got so damned late,
It missed a whole date.
Which made it early! – and truly sublime.

**THE LOZZLE SCHMOZZLE**

There was a trainee hoser who answered to Lozzle,
But, during the test, he used the wrong nozzle,
The spray went reverse,
The chief went perverse:

*"What, the fire truck?! ... This is quite the schmozzle!!!"*

## A RETRO SORRY AFFAIR

I'm so sorry that I'm compelled to be sorry,
To feed this strange 'victim state' of the pollie,
It's an insatiable need,
Be it sex, race or creed,
Bearing the guilt of *others* is a dangerous folly.

**THE SPRING THAT WENT PING**

There is a famous pole vaulter, Miss Tanding,
Who has yet to come in for her landing,
They confused her pole with a spring,
Then, with an almighty ***PING!***,
She was last sighted by the Sherpa called Tenzing.

**DeFAMED BUT NOT FORGOTTEN**

There was a politician called Danny DeFame,
Who was known to make claim after claim,
But like a big ball of gas,
He was gone in a flash,
When he got too close to a small naked flame.

## MAKING CRIME DISAPPEAR

There was a man who was quite clearly caught,
Stealing something he should rather have bought,
But a loophole was found,
For the law is not sound,
The time served?  A big, hefty nought.

**THE SPACE RACE**

My metabolism is losing its pace,
I have six chins that hang from my face,
I could say I'm 'big boned',
But NASA just phoned,
I've been spotted, from out there in Space.

**IN 3, 2 AND 1 ...**

Here is the story of poor Jenny McGee,
Who so desperately needed to pee,
She was the star of the show,
But she just had to go,
These are the perils of being *'live'* on TV.

## DEAD RINGER

Red Ringer was the gun pilot ace,
Shooting the enemy at world record pace,
While the battle was fought,
He viewed it as sport,
Until he *lost* ... and disappeared without trace.

**HERE'S LOOKING AT YOU KIDS**

As you step out into the wide open spaces,
You'll find more cameras are watching than faces,
So smile, brush 'n comb,
For your image is known,
To security types in *very* high places.

**PAY ME TV**

My new TV has *three thousand* channels,
Even the remote's got seventeen panels,
But wherever I go,
It's a rather drab show,
(*Hmm* ... might be time to get out of the flannels.)

## SHOO BOY

I know it can be quite the fight,
To keep the dreaded 'black dog' out of sight,
But make yourself smile,
If just for a while,
And ever so slowly, you'll start to feel right.

## THE TELEMARKETING BLITZKRIEG

They call and try to win my support,
For a thing not imagined - or sought,
But no longer doubt it,
*I can't live without it!*
(Though my banker looks somewhat distraught).

**LIVING IN THE SPAM OF PLENTY**

My Inbox is just so packed with spam,
There's barely room for a Nigerian scam,
But with this Dutch lottery win,
My ship has come in,
And my bags are packed for a life on the lam.

## LIFE FROM THE FACTORY FLOOR

There are those who work hard all their day,
In return for a set rate of pay,
While the profits head back,
To some lazy fat cat,
Floating around, in a yacht on the bay.

### *... MEANTIME, FROM THE CORNER OFFICE*

There are those who will call me a knob,
They're quick with a serve and a lob,
They don't want to be boss,
Battling profit 'n loss,
And for my 'sins' ... well, I provide them a job.

**YAPPY BUT HAPPY**

At the front door: man's best friend, on a mat,
Barking with a relentless and sharp *rat 'a tat*,
The neighbours despair,
But it's probably fair,
Because - let's be honest - at least it isn't a *cat*.

## I'M SO SOCIAL

The whole world 'friends' me with the click of a mouse,
I have thousands who think I'm quite grouse,
I'm big on the Twit,
Plus I get poked a bit,
And all of this without leaving the house.

**THE FREE TRADE SPIEL**

As governments shake hands and spruik trade,
For too many lives, the future's "un-made",
A sweat-shop *base rate*,
Seals everyone's fate,
If only the shakers, themselves, were waylaid.

## THE GOOD OLD TODAYS

We gripe and moan that *today* is a pest,
The 'golden era' is not our behest,
But the more that you grow,
Looking back you will know,
*Right now* is as good as the rest.

**TO SMILE THE IMPOSSIBLE SMILE**

My wife has become an important historical figure,
An international 'standard' of exceptional vigour,
The reason you see,
Despite the best jokes from me,
She's *humour immune* – and won't even snigger!

**SEE WILLY**

Getting fat's one thing, but this is quite silly,
Even my shins are becoming too hilly,
I can't touch my toes,
And down there ... *well who knows*,
I need three mirrors just to find dear old Willy!

## THE BALLAD OF EL GRINGO

Poor Maple arrived on the tour as a Gringo,
The cabbie knew she had none of the lingo,
They went here – they went there,
They ran up a huge fare,
Now Maple's strung out, chasing wins on 'el bingo'.

**PUT TO THE SWORD**

The high flying firm of Weezle & Sword,
Were known experts at suing for fraud,
Seems you are what you know,
They got caught on a 'stow',
And, henceforth, have been struck from the Board.

**SELFISH SELF-SABOTAGE**

There are mass sackings on the factory floors,
Creating a crisis locked away behind doors,
An economy made crappy,
To keep shareholders happy,
And overpaid fools who blindly keep score.

## CRASHING THROUGH THE CUBICLE BARRIER

I remember the day the Internet went out on our floor,

The Comfort Index crashed right down to 4,

First slow, then a surge,

People began to emerge,

And I found my *true love* - in the grey cube next door.

**TIGHT ON THE HEIGHT**

There was a high-walker who saw all the sights,
Till the day he got scared of the heights,
T'was a really close thing,
But he was saved by a string,
That had frayed in his triple-stitch tights!

**THE BALL 'O WONDER**

I've found a golf ball made of wondrous stuff,
It goes straight when the going gets tough,
It cannot be lost,
And came at no cost,
For I found it - *over there* - in the rough.

**KISS MY APPS**

The latest gadgets ensure I don't go amiss,
And prevent my 'rep' from copping a diss,
Without 'em today,
I'd sure go astray,
But without upgrades – behold! - *The Abyss*.

**TELEMARKETER REVENGE**

At the end of the day there was nowhere to recover,
The sellers attacked before I'd found cover,
But things are now fine,
I got an *extra* phone line,
So they're happily 'taking it out' on *each other*.

**AT THE END OF MY WICK**

Of birthdays, I've become somewhat lax,
There are candles in stacks upon stacks,
It's been such a long life,
I need a ginormous knife,
To find a cake 'neath this big ball of wax.

## McFAYLER THE INHALER

Paddy McFayler be famous at holding his bret',
And once outlasted the play of Macbet',
But, aye, when he let go,
T'was quite the big show,
*To be sure* - he shot over da cast, and da set.

## THE LEGEND OF THE DAREDEVIL JIMMY FORBITT

This is the legend of Jumpin' Jimmy Forbitt,

Short in stature but not scared of an ore pit,

But for his world record gamble,

They had too much angle,

And we're not sure when he'll be back ... from the orbit.

**EYE-BREAKER**

The tennis crowd was losing its voice and was losing its mind,

Abusive language had seen everyone fined,

But history was made,

With the players re-paid,

When tests found the umpire to be clinically blind.

**RED AHEAD**

My car is red and does 200 plus,
In auto circles it's made quite the fuss,
But with the limits round here,
I'm in second gear,
And being outpaced by a whopping great bus.

**SECOND OPINION**

I'm seeking a second opinion about my insides,
Not that I think my Doctor was telling me lies,
But you *are* slightly thrown,
And feeling alone,
When he diagnoses ... then just, up and dies.

**WRITTEN IN THE STARS**

My future's written right there in the stars,
Tall, dark strangers in all the right bars,
On the cusp of Uranus,
I'll be rich. I'll be famous,
So now I'm just waiting on Venus and Mars.

**THE GRAVITY OF DIGGING TOO DEEP**

Old Harris was a dab hand at digging for oil,
He'd pick the spot then he'd toil and he'd toil,
But he fell right off the Earth,
When he cut through its girth,
Dangling upside down – and plumb out of soil.

**D-I-Y ON THE FLY**

Why pay a huge sum when I feel I can try,
My own hand at some smart D-I-Y,
But the wife needs a tissue,
Cause my skills are an issue,
And the roof shows a fair bit of sky.

**THE HIDDEN WINNER**

The bedroom posters her own Hall of Fame,
Young Jenny finally went off to a game,
She learned more than it cost,
When her team took a loss,
For life would never be quite the same.

At first, she took it all straight to heart,
But came to learn that in sport, work or art,
The real rank of a 'win',
Comes deep from within,
To change who you are, when you *next* face the start.

Jenny learned there's no champ who's never been down,
And had to drag themselves back off the ground,
So, for the ultimate score,
Push yourself from the floor,
And in *fighting back*, real strength will be found.

## MAYOR TWO-FACE TYRONE

Two-Face Tyrone had his cell number tattooed on his chest,

Before being released at the Guv'nors behest,

He then ran for office,

Two-Face was no novice.

He said: "I've bunked with *and learned from* the best!"

## LANKY GOES TO GROUND

Lanky McKranksy could lift six times his own weight,

But this very skill would seal the man's fate,

For the stage turned to matches,

And the latest despatches,

Say Lanky now stands *'nearer three foot and eight'*.

**FIRST CLASS PASS**

Like a lottery win - I scored an airline upgrade,

Not only did I have my own butler - I had my own maid!

A night-time story was read,

A fluffy pillow for my head,

Meanwhile back in 'Cattle': *blankets and tempers all frayed.*

## HOUSTON WE HAVE A PROBLEM

Buzz Astro was made of all the right stuff,
But NASA gave him way *more* than enough,
Of a food that made smell,
Now, in a module, that's hell,
The crew found re-entry particularly rough.

**RENOVATOR'S DELIGHT**

This is your chance at a true renovator's delight,
Most take a peek, and then they take flight,
But with a bang and a bash,
And a mountain of cash,
You never know – you *may* stop that lean to the right.

**SWINGIN' CATS**

Our house is so small you can't swing a cat,
It's true – because we've actually tried that,
The RSPCA,
Said we needed to pay,
Let's just hope they don't look *too close* at the mat.

**THE GOOD OLD BLAZE**

Back in the day fireworks were *real* dynamite,
You could light up the sky from deep in the night,
But if you decided to linger,
You'd farewell a finger,
As the letterbox blew clean out of sight.

**QUICK DASH – GREAT SPLASH**

If you're nervous about the swim being chilled,
Here's the way to have your fear quickly stilled,
Sprint – don't think twice,
Convince yourself *it's like ice*,
Then only rarely will your dread be fulfilled.

**WIRE LIAR**

The Prosecution called him the Devil in Disguise,
Accused of telling a pack of big 'porkie pies',
He took a lie detector test,
But came out the best,
As no-one saw him cut the truth down to size.

In fact, he'd secretly *snipped* the blue wire,
To thwart the accusers who'd called him a liar,
But a short-circuit spark,
Brought an end to the lark,
Because then his pants really did catch on fire.

## NO NEWS IS BAD NEWS

Sadly, the news is no more worth the fuss,
It comes to here on an interstate bus,
Our local voice lost,
To penny-pinching cost,
What's the point when it's all *them* - and not us.

**DUELO EL UNO**

The duel had been set to take place after dawn,
But someone hit 'snooze', in the midst of a yawn,
With no opponent about,
An angry shot soon rang out,
Peppering the pillow, from way down on the lawn.

**A REELY LONG WALK**

Sam wasn't for walking dogs when he could also sleep in,

But the yappers persisted with an almighty din,

So with the longest fish pole,

They got out for their stroll,

As Sammy laid back – and then reeled 'em in.

## THE OLD THANKSGIVING FEUD

The thanksgiving feud's been so long and so dirty,
That its origins have become somewhat murky,
Fingers have been pointed,
And villains anointed,
But we know it started 'way back' with a turkey.

The McCoys claim their prize-winning bird,
Disappeared on November the third,
To be seen on a plate,
On the Thanksgiving date,
Although the Hatfield's say: *Simply absurd!*

The version from the old Hatfield clan,
Is their opponents were well 'on the lam',
And this cunning decoy,
Was a ploy from McCoy,
For the *Hatfield's* say they only ever ate ham.

The whereabouts of the gobbler: *'unknown'*,
But the standoff was soon overblown,
For with just the wrong snigger,
And a real itchy trigger,
The fate of the clans had truly been sown.

**THE BIG SPIN**

Whether it's my CDs, my Walkman, or my vinyl,
Too many formats have been deemed to be final,
It's quite the great rort,
The same stuff gets *re-bought*,
To keep hearing Elvis, The Big O and Lionel.

## THE TORSO TAX

The taxman suddenly arrived at my door,

And said: "Sorry, but we need a bit more",

They had an arm and a leg,

So it was off with my head,

They're back for my shadow, when they find the right saw.

**SAMMY THE SQUIRT**

Sammy Squirt was as quick as a spark,
In 12 seconds he could circle the park,
When it got to the night,
He'd flick out the light,
And be snoring before it got dark.

**STUMPY's SHORT SHRIFT**

This is the sad tale of poor Stumpy Hust
A pirate runner the fans could not trust,
His peg legs would need,
To blur at warp speed,
Till his shorts would spontaneously combust.

**GROUPIE SECTS**

Smooth Charlie has five women on the go,
How he does it, I simply don't know,
He's not that good looking,
And he's hopeless at cooking,
But, let's face it – he has the *lay-dee mo-jo*.

**GREEN SHOULD MEAN GO**

I've invented the world's most sustainable car,
But, alas, it doesn't go very far,
It winds-up like a toy,
And with that spinnaker, ahoy!
Top speed, *three knots* (on down-sloping tar).

## GOING THE EXTRA FOOD MILE

I like the notion of food that's organic,
Though the proponents seem a trifle too manic,
About pesticide spray,
And with the 'source', I must say,
Do these beans taste a little *Hispanic*?

**SWEEPSTAKES WINNER**

The magazine sweepstakes have just let me know,
There's only three hundred and five draws to go,
We're in the 20$^{th}$ year,
And my one greatest fear,
Is that I'll win it ... from round six feet below.

**CAPTAIN TURBULENCE**

Next time you're on a flight and food starts to appear,
And about the moment you reach out for that beer,
Before you can gooble,
The joystick will wobble,
*Captain Turbulence* is more common than queer.

**HOLE IN THE HEAD**

I remember being chuffed with my fine billy cart,
300 nails stopped it from falling apart,
But as I found to my dread,
There was one near my head,
Discovered on the big hill – just after the start.

**SHAKIN' ALL OVER**

This is the sorry tale of mis-matched Sally Payte,
A driving instructor whose nerves were not great,
But rather than a sacking,
They gave her their backing,
Which would've worked ... had she only gone straight.

**FAILING THE TEST OF TIME**

I have some shirts that are older than my lads,
Including the ones with the big shoulder pads,
But the one with the collar,
Makes the crowd point and holler,
Every damned 'comeback' has dodged all my fads!

## TAKE EM OUT & FILL ER UP

I decided that the bowser was trying to kid me,
But from Paris, to Rome and to Sydney,
With politics and tax,
Petrol's pushed to the max,
A full tank costs an arm and a kidney.

**DIMINISHING RETURNS**

Not so long back I was a true business Master,

Step out of the way, or be sure, I would blast ya,

But then things got too tight,

And with more wrinkles in sight,

The cheques have got slower and the bills have got faster.

**HERE IS THE SHOES**

We want newsreaders with cred and with style
As they tell us their stories so vile,
But below the desk tops,
Can be jeans and old socks,
Dwell on *that* little pic for a while!

**THE AUDITION REPETITION MISSION**

To be frank, every day should be called an audition,
An ongoing war of natural attrition,
Having experience is fine,
But respect's in decline,
You're only as safe as the very next mission.

**THE BOOK THAT WENT BOOM**

The publisher was quite the fanatic,
He was obsessed with the core demographic.
*"We need a book that goes 'boom',*
*That shakes up the room,*
*Now go off and write something fantastic!"*

I was determined to make him much prouder,
And being literal, I found some gunpowder,
With a spring it was sprung,
The boobytrap was all done,
Hell, the first page couldn't get any louder!

It may well be the greatest myst'ry,
In literature's long 'n chequered hist'ry,
You'll never know the conclusion,
For now I'm held in seclusion,
See you later – I hope that you'll miss me!

## THE BOOK HAS BEEN LOOKED

At the end of the book we've arrived,
I hope my words were not too contrived.
And that they made you feel good,
Because, you know, so they should,
*Now get out there! Let 'em know you're alive!*

For a good limerick is all about fun,
On a rainy day ... or out in the sun,
With a smile on your dial,
Enjoy life for a while,
OK – that's it – now get up off your bum.

To contact the author, or to check out the author's other books, visit www.vividpublishing.com.au/drx

www.ingramcontent.com/pod-product-compliance
Lightning Source LLC
Chambersburg PA
CBHW031408040426
42444CB00005B/471